Ashwin Dhivakar

To implement a Multi-level Security in Cloud Computing using Cryptography Novel Approach

Security in Cloud Computing

GRIN Verlag

Bibliografische Information der Deutschen Nationalbibliothek:

Die Deutsche Bibliothek verzeichnet diese Publikation in der Deutschen National-
bibliografie; detaillierte bibliografische Daten sind im Internet über http://dnb.d-
nb.de/ abrufbar.

Imprint:

Copyright © 2014 GRIN Verlag GmbH
Druck und Bindung: Books on Demand GmbH, Norderstedt Germany
ISBN: 978-3-656-65199-4

This book at GRIN:

http://www.grin.com/en/e-book/273465/to-implement-a-multi-level-security-in-
cloud-computing-using-cryptography

To implement a Multi-level Security in Cloud Computing using Cryptographic Novel approach

A Dissertation Proposal

Submitted

By

Ashwin Dhivakar M R

to

Department of Computer Science & Engineering

In Partial Fulfillment of the Requirement for the

Award of the Degree of

Master of Technology in Computer Science & Engineering

Lovely Professional University

Phagwara (Punjab)

(April, 2014)

DECLARATION

I hereby declare that the dissertation proposal titled, **To implement a multi-level security in Cloud Computing using a cryptographic novel approach** submitted for the M.Tech degree is entirely my genuine and original work. Entire Proposed work, research ideas and references have been duly acknowledged. It does not contain for the award of any other degree or diploma.

Date: 12/04/2014   Investigator

i

CERTIFICATE

This is to certify that Ashwin Dhivakar M R has completed M.Tech dissertation proposal titled **To implement a multi-level security in Cloud Computing using cryptographic novel approach** under my guidance and provision. To the best of my knowledge, the present work is the result of his original investigation and study. No part of dissertation proposal has been submitted for any other degree or diploma.

The dissertation proposal is fit for the submission and the partial fulfillment of the condition for the award of M.Tech Computer Science and Engineering.

Date: 12/04/2014   Signature of Advisor

ABSTRACT

Currently cloud computing environments have come up with a serious problem known as security which is in terms of Confidentiality of Data, Integrity of the Message and Authenticity of the users (CIA). Since user's personal data is being stored in an unencrypted format on a remote machine operated by third party vendors who provide various services, the impact of user's identity and unauthorized access or disclosure of files are very high. Though we have various techniques and algorithms to protect our data from hackers and intruders still cloud environments are prone to other attacks. In this paper, a novel approach is implemented to protect user's confidential data from third party service providers, and also to make sure that the data is not disclosed to any unauthentic user or the service provider even, in any cloud environments. This approach provides a multi-level security in three aspects: 1) User authentication for "authorization" to enter the network, 2) Image Sequencing password for "authentication" wherein it is proved that the identity is original user, and 3) RSA algorithm to encrypt the data further for providing "data integrity". Thus this approach provides an overall security to the client's personal data and the major issue of confidentiality, integrity and authenticity is fully solved. Implemented results are represented to illustrate that our approach has a reasonable performance.

ACKNOWLEDGEMENT

First of all, I am thankful to God for his blessings and showing me the right direction. With His mercy, it has been made possible for me to reach so far. It gives me great pleasure to express my gratitude towards the guidance and help I have received from **Mr. Parveen kumar**. I am thankful for his continual support, encouragement and invaluable suggestion. He not only provided me help whenever needed, but also the resources required to complete this Dissertation report on time. I am also thankful to **Prof. Dalwinder Singh,** Head, Computer Science and Engineering Department for his kind help and cooperation. I express my gratitude to all the staff members of Computer Science and Engineering Department for providing me all the facilities required for the completion of my Dissertation Proposal work. I would like to say thanks to the **Project Approval Committee members** for their valuable comment and discussion. I extend my thanks to **Lovely Professional University** for the support on academic studies and letting me involve in this study. I want to express my appreciation to every person who contributed with either inspirational or actual work to this Dissertation Proposal. Last but not the least I am highly grateful to all my family members for their inspiration and ever encouraging moral support, which enables me to purse my studies.

Ashwin Dhivakar M R

Registration No: 11200955

iv

Table of Contents

List of Figures

CHAPTER 1
INTRODUCTION

1.1 Cloud Computing

In the last few years there is an impressive change in computational power, storage and network communication technologies. These changes let human beings to generate, process, and share huge sets of information and data. Cloud computing is acted as the large pool, inside which there are various accessible and virtualized resources, these resources includes, hardware, development platforms and services. [3] Now, it is feasible to assemble any amount of powerful systems that consists of many small and low-cost service components since computers are at a very less price and compatibility is high these days with many technical advancements. Cloud computing provides huge techniques such as IT as a service. Cloud Computing provides services over internet, data and its applications are supported via remote servers, as:

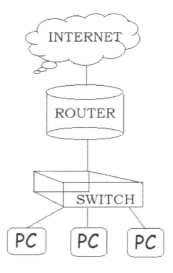

Figure 1.1: cloud computing internet structure

1

Cloud computing permits many user to access the system without installation of system files on any computer but it has to be connected on an internetwork. In Cloud computing, specific systems are required for executing applications on server and websites [4]. The cloud computing flexibility depends on authorization request for resources allocation and the act of uniting. Cloud computing is the emerging technology which is used to provide a range of storage services via the Internet [5]. It mainly has infrastructure, platform, and software as a service. These service provider lease information centric hardware's and software's to distribute storage and computing services over the network. Online users can be given services from a cloud like a super computer which is being used by cloud computing to store data on the cloud instead of storing on their device and access to data is possible anytime. Applications can run on powerful cloud computing platforms with software deployed on the cloud which justifies that the consumers are not in need for any software installation and upgrades on their local devices continuously.

1.2 History of Cloud Computing

In **1950**, the cloud computing concept came into picture. Here, the large scale mainframe computers are used in many corporations and these computers are accessible by the terminal computers. Time sharing is the process of sharing CPU time on a mainframe system.

In **1960-1990**, the present day scenario of the cloud computing, square measure explored by politician Parkhill, he described "The Challenge of the PC Utility". An agency Corporation was found in 1957. The Tymshare was found in 1966, National CSS was found in 1967 and acquired by Dun & poet in 1979, Dial information bought by Tymshare in 1968, and Bolt, Beranek and Newman BBN marketed time-sharing as a billboard venture.

In **1990**, telecommunications companies begin to offer virtual private network (VPN) services with good quality of service on a less price by switching traffic which suits a balanced server use; wherein bandwidth was efficiently used. They started using the cloud representation to indicate the segregation point. Network infrastructure and servers were bounded through cloud computing. [10]

In 2000, following the dot-com bubble, modernization of information centres were done by Amazon that was important within the evolution of cloud computing. A product was

2

launched for external customers and Amazon net Services (AWS) for computing supported utility in 2006. In 2008, Eucalyptus was the first open supply, AWS API-compatible platform for deploying personal clouds. In early 2008, Open Nebula was the first ASCII text file software package for deploying personal and hybrid clouds. On March 1, 2011, IBM declared the IBM sensible Cloud framework to support Smarter Planet. Amidst a variety of parts for Smarter Computing foundation, cloud computing could be an essential piece. On June 7, 2012, Oracle declared the Oracle Cloud. Despite the very fact that Oracle Cloud square measure still below improvement, this cloud is taken into account to be the first to supply users through access to AN integrated set of IT solutions, like Applications (SaaS), Platform (PaaS), and Infrastructure (IaaS) layers.

1.3 Service Models in Cloud Computing

1. Platform as-a Service (PaaS): In PaaS, the clients obtain access to platforms, which enables users to deploy their personal software and applications on the cloud. The customer doesn't manage the network or OS either but are limited to the type of applications [12].

2. Infrastructure as-a Service (IaaS): Here the Network connections, storage and applications are controlled and executed by clients. Communications as a Service model is used to depict hosted IP telephony services. To avoid the expenses and a dedicated system which provides all resources for computing environment a physical infrastructure is really distant.

3. Software as-a service (SaaS): Software as a service is an outlet for delivering the service over Internet and it runs thousands of customers on a single deployment code which means if we fix a problem for one customer then it is fixed for everyone on the network, it may also use open APIs and web services for integration but every client has to pay for what is used on the cloud.

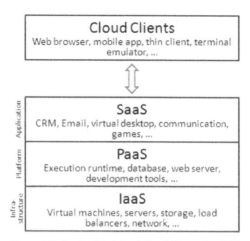

Figure 1.2: Service Models of Cloud Computing [13]

1.4 Deployment Models of Cloud Computing

Deploying cloud computing depends upon the different requirements; hence it is different from each other. As for deploying a cloud computer, four deployment models can be used. Each model has its specific characteristics.

1. Private Cloud: The private cloud is used for the personal work, some organizations can maintain specifically on a private cloud. The operation takes place either at clients or at third party's side.

2. Community Cloud: This cloud is shared amongst the various Companies. These organizations have the same interests and requirements.[3] These requirements help to limit the capital costs for its establishment.

3. Public Cloud: The cloud infrastructure is offered to the general public on a billboard basis by a cloud service supplier. This allows a client to develop and deploy a service within the cloud with little or no money outlay compared to the cost necessities.

4. Hybrid Cloud: The cloud infrastructure consists of variety of clouds of any sort; however the clouds have the power through their interfaces to permit knowledge or applications to be moved from one cloud to a different. This may be a mix of personal and public clouds.

4

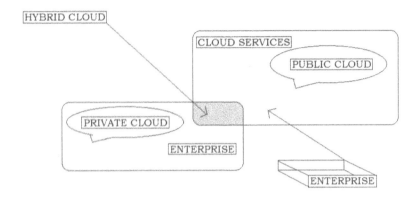

Figure 1.3: Public, Private, and Hybrid Cloud Deployment

1.5 Benefits of cloud computing

There are many benefits of the cloud computing, these benefits are based upon the services and applications of the cloud computing.

• **Scalability:** The cloud computers are scalable in nature. The organizations initially can run on a small deployment model and later they can even adapt to larger models and if it needed, they can even scale back to its initial state if necessary.

• **Flexibility:** The flexibility in the cloud environment provides organizations to utilize the resources whenever the customer demands for additional features. To convince a customer the flexibility of the resources is needed.

• **Cost Savings:** cloud computing helps the organization to reduce their capital expenditures.

• **Reliability:** cloud computing is more reliable because the services used in this having multiple redundant sites. These sites support the business continuity.

• **Maintenance:** The cloud system provides the maintenance. It does not require any application installation on the PC, the access of the system done through APIs directly.

• **Mobile Accessible:** These systems are accessible in any infrastructure. Hence cloud system help to increase the productivity of the system.

1.6 Challenges of Cloud computing

There are many challenges that are associated with cloud computing.

1. Security and Privacy: In the cloud computing data storage and data security is important aspects. The cloud [3] computing can be monitor by the service providers.

2. Lack of Standards: In the cloud computing, clouds have standard interfaces. Hence there are no standards related to cloud computing. To resolve these issues open cloud computing interface is comes into picture; it helps to resolve many issues. [8]

3. Continuously Evolving:

The requirements of the user are continuously evolving, hence requirements for interfaces, networking and storage is increased and decreased according to the need of person. This means that a cloud behave dynamically.

4. Compliance Concerns:

Cloud computing has many issues regarding its data protection. Its main concern is about the affecting factors of cloud computing. These factors make an impact on the data types and application for the purpose the cloud is utilized.

1.7 Cloud Computing with the Communications Services

In a cloud the communications services will extend their capabilities. It conjointly helps to provides new interactive capabilities to current services. These services change businesses to infix communications capabilities into business applications. The services of the cloud computing is accessed from any location and joined into current services to increase their capabilities, additionally as stand alone as service offerings.

1.8 Accessing through internet APIs

Accessing communications capabilities in an exceedingly cloud-based atmosphere is achieved through genus Apis. It permits the appliance development outside the cloud to require advantage of the communication infrastructure among it.

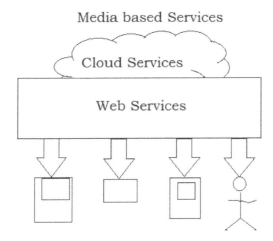

Figure 1.4: Web 2.0 Interfaces to the Cloud

1.9 Cloud Computing Trends for 2014

1. Cloud enables agility and business innovation: Now days, every business is a digital business. The world is changing, due to the increasing need of IT. Cloud computing supports the rapid experiments and innovation, hence is recognized as facilitating speed to market. The cloud solutions are used to help business to understand the customer unique challenges. [18]

2. Security, Addressing security & privacy is key to building trust in cloud computing: The cloud performance is depends upon its security. Everyone, who want to do work in cloud, he or she must check the security of cloud. There are various security issues in cloud namely.

• Physical Security and Data Location

• Network Security

• Backup & Recovery

• Operational Compliance

7

- Confidentiality & Integrity
- Data Portability
- Location of Data

3. System of Engagement - Common User Experience across delivery models, cloud as a wrapper

Cloud solutions are highly agile wrapper around different systems, different behavior. They help in bringing all together in an engagement cycle. Cloud computing also helps in changing the ways of interaction between the people and technology. It may lead in enabling new forms of consumer applications.

4. Cloud as the innovation platform – Mobile, Social, Big Data

Mobile is the mega trend of our century. It has become a commodity. Social has permeated through our personal and business networks. Big Data, the volume of data available for organizations to mine for business value is staggering. Cloud technology provides a common platform for Mobile, Social and Big Data applications to cross pollinate as well as enhance and extend existing investments.

5. Social: Collaboration in a business context: The Collaboration between generations of employees has to be transactional as well as provide business context for a successful knowledge transfer. The collaboration is embedded into the business process. Increasingly business processes will have many cloud touch points, making a case for cloud based collaboration.

6. Big Data – Actionable data: Big Data has become the catch, all phrase for the volume of data businesses generate today. Without appropriate action, the collection and analysis of the data is worthless. Cloud technology makes the collection, analysis and dissemination of results and actions that much easier due to its flexibility.

7. Real time and Predictive: Now a day, the real time is no longer enough, the real time also needs to be predictive. It is not about the advance analytics. A cloud platform and solutions will provide the base for such innovation and agility.

8. Networks - The business network effect: The Network effect only kicks in if you are open and you scale fast. It is simple, more users make a network more attractive and amplify the benefit for all.

8

9. Platform: you need to have a PaaS to succeed with cloud solutions. . A critical factor will be the ability of this platform to drive innovation as well as provide integration to your existing landscape.

10. Hybrid cloud: You cannot move everything to the cloud. You may not even want to.

1.10 CLOUD SECURITY THREATS

Cloud computing has many security threats. The files in the cloud computing is share by many users. Hence the confidentiality becomes the major issue in this case. There are many security threats in cloud computing, as: [20]

1. **Data Breaches:** The data breach biggest issue in case of cloud security. At the target the data breaches result in the loss of personal and credit card information of many users. If the database of cloud computing is not properly designed then there may be chances of attacker to attack the data. This may harmful to our whole system.

1. **Data Loss:** In a cloud computing, knowledge loss is occurring. The info is lost in several conditions, such as: once a hard drive dies while not its owner is having created a backup. The info loss may occur by choice within the event of a malicious attack.

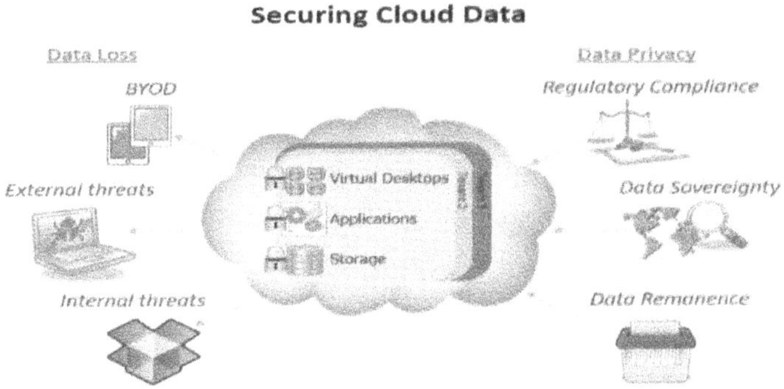

Figure 1.5: cloud computing threats [14]

9

2. Service Traffic Hijacking: The service hijacking is that the biggest issue in cloud computing. Phishing, exploitation of software package vulnerabilities and credentials will all cause the loss of management over a user account.

3. Insecure APIs: The application programming interface, (API), defines however a 3rd party connects associate degree application to the service and providing verification that the third party manufacturing the appliance.

4. Denial of Service: Denial of threat is an attack which is formulated to create a huge traffic over a network such that it gets harder to find between the legitimate user's request and intruder's message. It is considered as a threat since the delivery and acknowledgement of original packets are greatly affected.

5. Malicious Insiders: Inside a large cloud organization, the hazards are magnified. One tactic cloud customers should use to protect themselves is to keep their encryption keys on their own premises, not in the cloud.

6. Abuse of Cloud Services: Cloud computing brings large scale, elastic services to enterprise users and hackers alike. It might take attacker years to crack an encryption key using his own limited hardware.

7. Insufficient Due Diligence: There are many enterprises jump into the cloud without understanding the full scope of the undertaking. Without an understanding of the service providers' environment and protections, customers don't know what to expect in the way of incident response, encryption use, and security monitoring. Enterprises may push applications that have internal on-premises network security controls into the cloud, where those network security controls don't work.

8. Shared Technology: In a multi tenant environment, the compromise of a single component exposes more than just the compromised customer. The cloud is about shared infrastructure, and a mis-configured operating system. In a shared infrastructure, the CSA recommend an in-depth defensive strategy. Defenses should apply to the use of compute, storage, networking, applications, and user access.

9. Cloud Security Controls: The cloud security design will be acknowledging the problems that may arise with security management.

10. Deterrent controls: These controls are set in site to stop any eventful or purposeful attack on a cloud system

11. Preventative controls: These kinds of controls helps in change the strength of the system by managing the vulnerabilities.

12. Detective control: Detective controls are accustomed find any attacks which will be occurring to the system.

1.11 Advantages of cloud computing

1. Scalability: Cloud computing is scalable. Whenever user would like additional resources, the user will add it to anytime. That's the reason Cloud computing is infinite pool of resources.[23]

2. Environment friendly: Cloud computing just makes economical use of hardware and its resources which helps to cut back energy value.

3. Cost economical: Cloud computing is value economical. We've got to pay only for the quantity that we have used like utility bill.

4. Up to date: We need to not worry regarding the updates to the software's and hardware's that we have a tendency to be victimized within the cloud. The supplier is accountable for the update method of all the parts [2].

5. Improved performance: Whenever we want some high configuration resources it'll be on the market to the user on its demand.

6. Availability: The cloud service is distributed over multiple servers. The cloud systems will transfer the hosted applications close to instantly between these infrastructures. Therefore notwithstanding a server fails, the supply are nearly unscathed.

7. Coping with massive load variations: There are multiple servers and data centres of the cloud computing. If the applications of the cloud computing become extremely popular, the cloud infrastructure will not fall to its knees.

8. Timely and consistent updates: The cloud infrastructure is has to be totally in line with one another. There are running many shoppers applications, a failure because of a patch isn't

11

one thing the cloud service can settle for. Therefore all servers are terribly quick and systematically updated.

9. Extremely fast scaling out: If your application features a sustained high visit rate, it desires additional servers to run on. This can be terribly straightforward to implement in an exceedingly multi-server, multi-site atmosphere of a cloud service.

1.12   Disadvantages of Cloud Computing

1. Custom platform: The cloud service supplier styles the cloud service atmosphere with its specifics, like underlying software, databases, [1] application server and development platform. These are mounted across the whole cloud platform.

2. Lock in: Once the whole application is accommodates run on the cloud service atmosphere, it's going to be troublesome to makeover it to a different cloud service supplier. Here the user has got to readjust everything to run on the new cloud service.

3. Isolation breach: A breach between the isolation controls of various customers will cause access to proprietary information.

4. Data protection: Within the cloud computing, information is incredibly necessary. Typically information is incredibly confidential in nature. Since all this information is managed by the service supplier, incidents of information loss, information leaks and security breaches will all happen.

5. Cost: The cloud service suppliers have lots of innovative valuation mechanisms, like valuation per I/O, Bandwidth, or any combination of these. Therefore whereas potency and accessibility can definately increase, therefore might the prices is additionally multiplied. [5]

CHAPTER 2
LITERATURE SURVEY

1. Above the Trust and Security in Cloud Computing: A Notion towards Innovation, (Ahmed.M et.al, 2010): In this paper author discuss the safety of cloud computers. Cloud computing is for web computing. [9] the web is often envisioned as clouds. Cloud computing provides the ability to access shared resources and customary infrastructure, giving services on demand over the network to perform operations that meet dynamic business wants. The placement of physical resources and devices being accessed are usually not celebrated to the top user. This paper shows the varied cloud computing problems. To produce the simplest security to cloud computing author first of all derive a secure protocol by eliminating the support pitfalls that stay dormant. It will increase the confidentiality and integrity of knowledge that's price exchanging between the INO and also the CSP.

2. Architecture based on proactive model for security in cloud computing, (Srivastava.P et.al... 2011): In this paper, author discusses a proactive model for the safety of cloud computing. Cloud computing is outlined as a model for enabling convenient, on demand network access to a shared pool of configurable [10] computing resources that may be quickly provisioned and free with marginal management effort or service supplier interaction. The cloud technology could be a growing trend. Cloud Computing paradigm has one obvious problem: security, as a result of the cloud could be a new paradigm, it involves careful coming up with and execution. During research on this paper, we tend to analyze the safety landscape very well and propose design supported a proactive model that tackles this more and more tough downside in an exceedingly comprehensive manner. A Security Cloud actively monitors the Cloud Service supplier for policy violations.

3. Confidentiality Protection in Cloud Computing Systems (Stephen S. Yau et. al... 2010): In this paper, author discuss concerning the safety in cloud computing. As, cloud computing provides the web based mostly services. As web growth is will increase rapidly. Therefore cloud computing ends up in the vision of web as a mainframe. [11] There are several techniques for shielding user knowledge from outside attackers. Presently there exists no effective means for shielding user sensitive knowledge from service suppliers in cloud computing. In this paper, author presents a brand new approach to guard the confidentiality of knowledge within the cloud computing. In this paper, author doesn't contemplate confidentiality protection from attackers outside cloud computing systems.

4. Data Security and Privacy Protection Issues in Cloud Computing, (Chen.D et. al... [2010]): In this paper, author discuss concerning the problems in knowledge security and privacy protection. Today several organizations are realizing the advantages by golf shot their applications and knowledge into the cloud. The adoption of cloud computing might cause gains in potency and effectiveness in developing and preparation and save the value. [12] The cloud computing security issues to information security and privacy protection problems stay the first substance for adoption of cloud computing services. This paper provides a cryptic however all spherical analysis on knowledge security and privacy protection problems related to cloud computing across all stages of knowledge life cycle. Then this paper discusses some current solutions.

5. Ensuring Data Storage Security in Cloud computing using Sobol Sequence, (P. Syam Kumar et.al... 2010): In this paper author discuss concerning the info storage security in cloud computing. Cloud computing is a web primarily based computing. It delivers everything as a service over the web supported user demand.[8] These services square measure classified into 3 types:

• 	Infrastructure as a Service (IaaS)

• 	Platform as a Service (PaaS)

• 	Software as a Service (SaaS)

Cloud knowledge storage (Storage as a Service) is a vital service of cloud computing referred as Infrastructure as a Service (IaaS). Information storage in cloud offers such a large amount of advantages to users. Cloud computing provides great deal of computing and storage to customers provisioned as a service over the web. Cloud computing faces such a large amount of security challenges attributable to the numerous failures. In this paper, author target making certain knowledge storage security in cloud computing, that is a vital facet of Quality of Service. In this paper, author propose an efficient and versatile distribution verification protocol to deal with knowledge storage security in cloud computing. In this protocol,

14

erasure code for the availability, responsibleness and utilize token pre computation exploitation Sobol Sequence to verify the integrity of erasure coded data instead of pseudorandom information in existing system.

6. Ensuring Data Storage Security in Cloud Computing, (Wang.C et.al...): In this paper, author discuss concerning the info storage security in cloud computing. Cloud computing is AN Internet-based development. [13]   The increasing network information measure and reliable nevertheless versatile network connections create it even doable that users will currently subscribe prime quality services from knowledge and software package that reside entirely on remote knowledge centres. Cloud Computing isn't simply a 3rd party knowledge warehouse. The info hold on within the cloud is often updated by the users. Cloud Computing moves the applying software package and knowledge bases to the big data centers, wherever the management of the info and services might not be totally trustworthy. during this paper, a good and versatile distributed theme is purposed to confirm the correctness of user knowledge within the cloud.

7. Implementation of Data Security in Cloud Computing, (Jai Arul Jose1.G et. al... 2011): In this paper, author's main focus is on knowledge security in cloud computing. Within the cloud computing the info and applications exist on cloud of net servers. [14] Cloud computing systems are useful to divide these applications into 2 scenarios: within the front and also the side. All cloud computing systems don't have identical computer programme. All servers are run with its own freelance package. Cloud computing follows some set of rules known as protocols and uses a special reasonably software package, referred to as middleware. A cloud system makes a duplicate copy of all client's info and stores it on alternative devices. These copies enable the central server to access backup machines to retrieve knowledge. Cloud computing provides folks the thanks to share distributed resources and services that belong to totally different organizations. The cloud computing uses the web because the communication media. In this paper, author proposes a model system within which cloud system is combined with Cluster Load levelling.

8. Privacy-Preserving Public Auditing for Data Storage Security in Cloud Computing, (Wang.C, et. al... 2010): In this paper author discuss concerning the information storage security in cloud computing. The cloud computing is that the vision of computing as a utility,

15

wherever users will remotely store their knowledge into the cloud. Cloud Computing has been visualized because the next generation design of IT enterprise. Cloud Computing is remodelling the terribly nature of however businesses use info technology.[6] One elementary facet of this paradigm shifting is that knowledge is being centralized into the Cloud. During this paper author discuss concerning the info storage security. Because the knowledge of the user is extremely confidential in nature, that the knowledge security has the most concern in cloud computing. There are several security reasons within the cloud computing, as: the infrastructures below the cloud are a lot of powerful and reliable than personal computing devices. These devices face the each internal and external threat for knowledge integrity. There exist numerous motivations for cloud service suppliers to behave towards the cloud users relating to the standing of their outsourced knowledge. In this paper, author projected a privacy conserving public auditing system for knowledge storage security in Cloud Computing. during this author, utilize the homo morphed critic and random masking to ensure that TPA wouldn't learn any information concerning the information content hold on the cloud server throughout the economical auditing method. To support economical handling of multiple auditing tasks, the author more explore the technique of linear combination signature to increase main result into a multi-user setting, wherever TPA will perform multiple auditing tasks at the same time.

9. The Management of Security in Cloud Computing (Ramgovind. S, et. al... 2010): In this paper author discuss regarding the management of the cloud computing. Cloud computing may be a new and rising data technology that changes the means IT disciplined. Solutions are advocated by suggestions that of moving towards the theme of visualization of information storage, of native networks also as package Cloud computing [7] has elevated IT to newer limits by providing the market surroundings knowledge storage and capability with versatile climbable computing process power to match elastic demand and provide. Cloud computing will facilitate keep ones IT budget to a vacant minimum. Cloud computing will deliver a colossal array of IT capabilities in real time mistreatment many alternative varieties of resources like hardware, software, storage once logged onto a cloud. the aim of the paper is to supply associate overall security perspective of Cloud computing with the aim to spotlight the protection considerations that ought to be properly self-addressed and managed to appreciate the complete potential of Cloud computing.

10. Towards Trusted Cloud Computing, (Nuno Santos Krishna P.G, 2010): In this paper, author discuss concerning the trusty cloud computing. Firms will greatly cut back IT prices by offloading knowledge and computation to cloud computing services. So as to forestall confidentiality violations, cloud services' customers would possibly resort to secret writing. Secret writing is effective in securing knowledge before it's hold on at the supplier. Cloud pc cannot apply within the services wherever knowledge is to be computed. Cloud computing infrastructures modify firms to chop prices by outsourcing computations on-demand. To handle this downside [15] author proposes the look of a trusty cloud computing platform (TCCP). TCCP permits Infrastructure as a Service (IaaS) suppliers like Amazon EC2 to produce a closed box execution surroundings that guarantees confidential execution of guest virtual machines.

CHAPTER 3
PRESENT WORK

3.1 Problem Formulation

Now days, information security has been a vital issue in cloud computing environments. Clouds don't have any borders and therefore the information may be physically set anyplace in any information centre across the network geographically distributed. That the nature of cloud computing raises serious problems relating to user authentication, info integrity and confidentiality. With the cloud model, you lose management over physical security. In a public cloud, you're sharing computing resources with different corporations. In a shared pool outside the enterprise, you do not have any data or management of wherever the resources run. Storage services provided by one cloud seller could also be incompatible with another vendor services. Information integrity is assurance that the information is consistent and proper. Guaranteeing the integrity of the information very implies that it changes solely in response to licensed transactions. The cloud service supplier for cloud makes certain that the client doesn't face any drawback like loss information or data thievery. There's conjointly an opportunity wherever a malicious user will penetrate the cloud by impersonating a legitimate user, there by infecting the complete cloud.

3.2 Research Objectives

- To enhance the safety of the cloud computing
- Increase the integrity of information
- Increase the confidentiality of information
- To increase the cloud reliableness

3.3 Research Methodology

There are basic two types of attacks.
- Active attacks

- Passive attacks

In the passive attacks, the data which is confidential breaks, as in this case the third party only accesses your data but the third party cannot do any modification in the data.

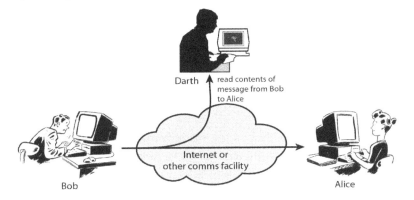

Figure 3.1: data confidentiality breaks [1]

In the active attacks, the data integrity breaks, the data can be modified by the third party and it can be sent back to the user.

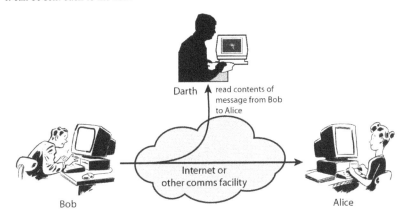

Figure 3.2: data integrity breaks [1]

To resolve the problem of security in cloud computing, we are going to use multi way security on cloud computing. Here image sequence base password provides security from authentication attacks at user end. RSA Algorithm use for secure encryption of data over our cloud

There is numerous security services employed in the cloud computing as:

• Authentication - assurance that the communication entity is that the one claimed

• Access management - hindrance of the unauthorized use of a resource

• Data Confidentiality –protection of information from unauthorized revelation

• Data Integrity - assurance that information received is as sent by a licensed entity

• Non-Repudiation - protection against denial by one among the parties in a communication

In our case, we are going to use the image sequencing password with RSA to enhance the security of cloud computing. Suppose in this we use the horse-cow-goat-panda. The sequence numbers of them are 2468. So when we enter the sequence number we are enter to the cloud.

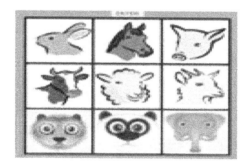

Figure 3.3: image sequencing

Here in the fig 3.4, the position of the animals are shuffle, hence our password is also change. Now our password becomes 4865 according to the position of horse-cow-goat-panda.

20

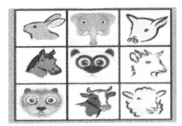

Figure 3.4: image shuffling.

We use the RSA formula as:

1. Select two prime numbers P and Q (any larger prime number)

2. Calculate the value N = P x Q

3. Choose the general public key (i.e, secret writing Key) E such it's not an element of (P-1) and (Q-1)

4. Choose the personal key (i.e, Decryption Key) D such the subsequent relative atomic mass is true:

$(D \times E) \bmod (P-1) \times (Q-1) = 1$

5. For encryption, calculate the cipher text CT from the plain text Pt as follows:

$CT = PT^E \bmod N$

6. Send CT back as the cipher text to the receiver

7. For decoding, calculate the plain Text Pt from the cipher text CT as follows:

$PT = CT^D \bmod N$

Example:

Key Generation:

1. Choose two distinct prime numbers P=61 and

Q=53.

2. Compute N=P*Q, thus N=61*53 = 3233.

3. Compute Euler's quotient function, $\emptyset(n)=(P-1)*(Q-1)$,

Thus $\emptyset(n)=(61-1)*(53-1) = 60*52 = 3120$.

4. Chose any integer e, such that $1 < e < 3120$ that is co-prime

21

to 3120. Here, we chose e=17.

5. Compute R , R = e-1(mod Ø(n)),

thus R=17-1(mod 3120) = 2753.

6. Thus the Public-Key is (e, n) = (17, 3233) and the Private- Key is (R, n) = (2753, 3233). This Private-Key is kept secret and it is known only to the user.

Encryption:

1. The Public-Key (17, 3233) is given by the Cloud service provider for user to store the data.

2. Let us consider that the user mapped the data to an integer m=65.

3. Data is encrypted using Cloud service provider by using Public-Key which is shared by both the service provider and the user.

C = 6517(mod 3233) = 2790.

4. This encrypted data i.e, cipher text is now stored by the Cloud service provider.

Decryption:

1. When the user requests the data, Cloud service provider will authenticate the user and delivers the encrypted data (If the user is valid).

2. The cloud user then decrypts the data by computing, m = Cd(mod n) = 27902753(mod 3233) = 65.

3. Once the m value is obtained, user will get back the original data.

CHAPTER 4
IMPLEMENTATIONS AND RESULT

1.11   Implementation

1. NetBeans

Figure 4.1: Cloud Sim And Net beans

In this case, we open net-beans, which is java based platform. To run the cloud systems just right click on the file system and click on run.

2. Wrong Password: In this case, a GUI page gets open. Here a window opens and I used it for the authentication purpose. In this case, if we enter wrong password, it shows the warning that the password you enter is wrong.

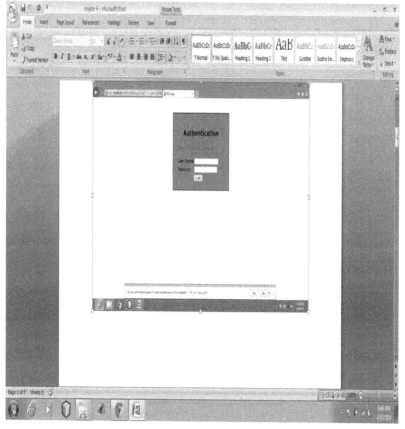

Figure 4.2: Wrong Password

24

3. Wrong User Name: In this case, if we give the wrong input in front of user name, then a warning appears to remind us that we have to enter the authorized user name.

Figure 4.3: Authentication

4. Warning Appears: In this case, if we don't provide the information regarding user name and password, it gives us the warning.

Figure 4.4: Warning Message

5. Go To Next Page: In this case, we enter in the cloud. If we want to store data in cloud, we have to match the password. This password is integrated to images and numeric values. This password is known as image sequencing password. If we write wrong password, it gives the warning that wrong password enter. It is unable to move to other platform.

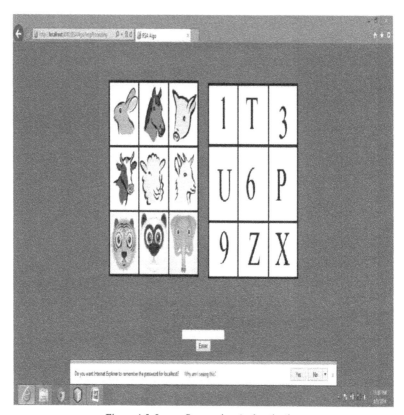

Figure 4.5: Image Sequencing Authentication

26

6. Enter Wrong Sequence: In this case, we enter in the cloud. If we want to store data in cloud, we have to match the password. This password is integrated to images and numeric values. This password is known as image sequencing password. If we write wrong password, it gives the warning that wrong password enter. It is unable to move to other platform.

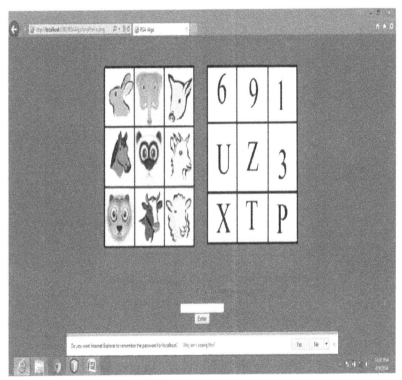

Figure 4.6: Wrong Sequence

7. Image shuffle: In this case, we enter in the cloud. If we want to store data in cloud, we have to match the password. This password is integrated to images and numeric values. This password is known as image sequencing password. If we write wrong password, it gives the warning that wrong password enter. It is unable to move to other platform. Here images are shuffle when we enter password each time.

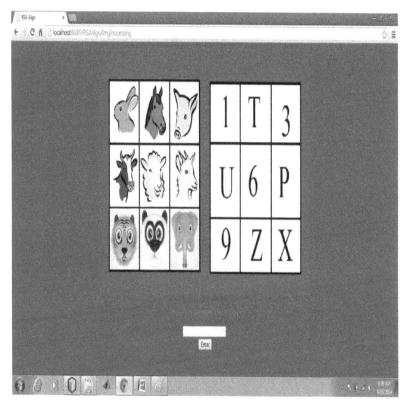

Figure 4.7: Image Shuffle

8. Enter Correct Pattern: In this case, we enter into cloud by entering the correct information. In this case, we can store the data in cloud and also we can retrieve the data.

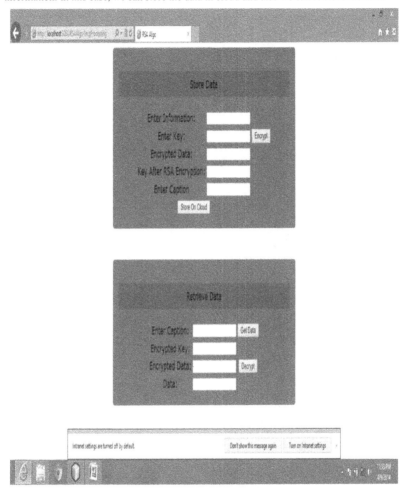

Figure 4.8: User Interface on Cloud

9. Enter the information: In this case, if we want to store the data in cloud computing, we have to enter information that we want to store in the cloud. Then we have to enter key. When we click on encrypt button, it encrypt the data and provide the key which is generated after applying RSA.

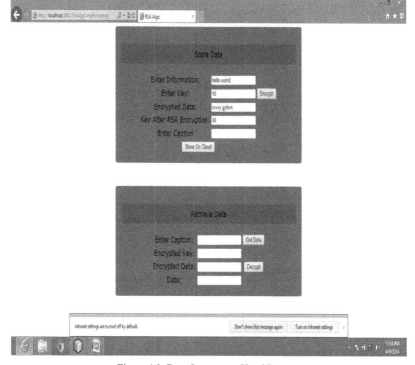

Figure 4.9: Data Storage on Cloud Process

10. Data Uploaded: After providing the information, when we click on Store on cloud, it stores the information on cloud.

30

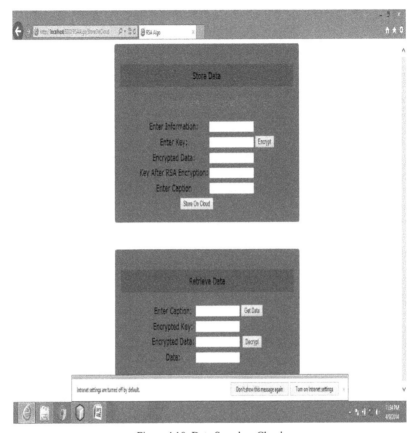

Figure 4.10: Data Saved on Cloud

2. **Data Retrieve:** In this case, if we want to retrieve the information from the cloud, firstly we add the caption, then the key which is generated after the use of RSA. Then we enter the encrypted data.

31

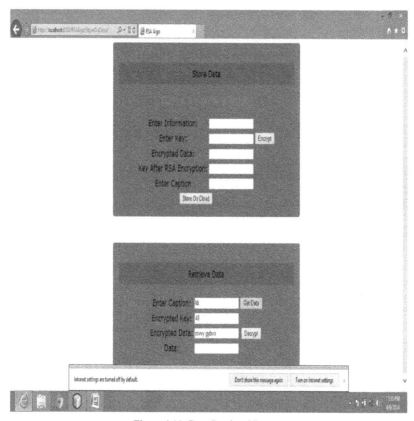

Figure 4.11: Data Retrieval Process

3.   Decryption: When we click on decrypt, it decrypts the information and shows us on the cloud system.

32

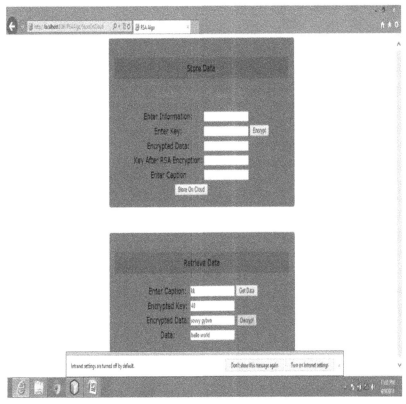

Figure 4.12: Decryption of Data

CHAPTER 5
CONCLUSION AND FUTURE SCOPE

In this project a complete examinations on protection techniques were analyzed and the proposed security hierarchy turns out to be a better algorithm than the current protection techniques. The issue of Confidentiality, Integrity and Authenticity is sorted out using this security algorithm which protects data from unauthorized user, disclosure of contents and data repudiation. Now the cloud service providers can adopt such techniques to attract more users and provide them any type of services in a much secured environment.

[1]   Stallings, William, "Public Key Encryption and RSA," in Cryptography and Network Security, 5th ed. Published by Pearson Education, Inc, Copyright © 2011, pp. 293-314.

[2]   John W. Rittinghouse, James F. Ransome, "Web Services Delivered from the Cloud," in Cloud Computing Implementation, Management, and Security", *CRC Press Taylor & Francis Group 6000 Broken Sound Parkway NW, Suite 300 Boca Raton, FL 33487-2742,* Copyright © 2010 by Taylor and Francis Group, LLC, pp. 48-95.

[3]   Somani, Lakhani. K, Mundra. M, "Implementing digital signature with RSA encryption algorithm to enhance the Data Security of cloud in Cloud Computing, "in *Proc. Parallel Distributed and Grid Computing (PDGC), 2010 1st International Conference, Solan, 28-30 Oct 2010, pp.211-216.*

[4]   AlZain, Soh, Pardede, "Using Multi-clouds to Ensure Security in Cloud Computing, "in Proc. Dependable, Autonomic and Secure Computing (DASC), 2011 IEEE Ninth International Conference, Sydney, 12-14 Dec. 2011, pp. 784 - 791.

[5]   Wentao Liu, Dept. of Comput. & Inf. Eng., Wuhan Polytech. Univ., Wuhan, China "Research on cloud computing security problem and strategy, "in *Proc. Consumer Electronics, Communications and Networks (CECNet), 2012 2nd International Conference, Yichang, 21-23 April 2012, pp. 1216 - 1219.*

[6]   Wang Cong, "Privacy-Preserving Public Auditing for Data Storage Security in Cloud Computing", IEEE TRANSACTIONS ON COMPUTERS, VOL. 62, NO. 2, FEBRUARY 2013 pg 362-372

[7]   Kumar Syam, R. Subramanian and D. Thamizh Selvam ,Ensuring Data Storage Security in Cloud Computing using Sobol Sequence, 2010 1st International Conference on Parallel, Distributed and Grid Computing (PDGC - 2010) pg 217-223

[8]   Ahmed Mahbub, et.al, Above the Trust and Security in Cloud Computing: A Notion towards Innovation, 2010 IEEE/IFIP International Conference on Embedded and Ubiquitous Computing Pg 723-730

[9]   Srivastava Prashant et.al, An architecture based on proactive model for security in cloud computing, IEEE-International Conference on Recent Trends in Information Technology, ICRTIT 2011 IEEE MIT, Anna University, Chennai. June 3-5, 2011

[10] Stephen S. Yau and Ho G, An Confidentiality Protection in Cloud Computing Systems, Int J Software Informatics, Vol.4, No.4, December 2010, pp. 351-365.

[11] G. Jai Arul Jose1, C. Sajeev2, Dr. C. Suyambulingom, Implementation of Data Security in Cloud Computing, International Journal of P2P Network Trends and Technology-Volume1Issue1- 2011 pp. 240-243.

[12] www.azurecloudpro.com

[13] www.greenclouds.uk

[14] www.computingcloudstorage.com